A.R.E Y.O.U F.R.E.E

Moving forward after divorce

Cherise Parker

I am grateful that you purchased this book. My hope is that what you read gives you a little more strength to keep pressing on. Please know that you are not alone in this, with time you will get through. My desire is that this gives you the push to begin again!

You will see as you dive into the book that I have added pages for you to journal your process. Journaling really helped me to process everything I was going through. This allowed me to release what I was feeling, and not keep it bottled in. Now I can look back on it and no longer feel the hurt attached to it and see where God has brought me. He brought me from a place of despair to dignity and He will do the same for you.

Love you so very much.
Your sister in Christ,

Published by I AM Publishing, LLC

Copyright© 2016 by I AM Publishing, LLC

All rights reserved. Absolutely no part of this book may be reproduced, store in or introduced into a retrieval system, or transmitted in any form or by any means without the expressed written consent of the Publisher or the Author of this book, Violators will be prosecuted to the full extent of the law.

For information regarding special discounts for bulk purchases or to have Cherise speak at your event please contact an I AM M.E. representative cherise@madeexcellent.com or 949-542-6782

Acknowledgements

I want to thank God for loving me when I did not love myself; for choosing me and creating me to be something that I never thought I could be. I thank Him for preparing me for this very moment in time.

I am thankful to each and every person that said "There is a book in you Cherise," and "Write the book Cherise." Special thanks to the Purpose Passion Profit (formerly the Grow Your Dreams Network) Conference 2018 speakers that ignited the fire in me to finally complete this book.

Jayla, Devin, and Benjamin I love you so very much! Thank you for showing me that love never fails. To my family and friends thank you for your support and encouragement…and to you my KING thank you for opening my eyes to something new and allowing my heart to feel true love.

Introduction

When you get married the hope is to live out the "til death do us part" and the "happily ever after." Well for me that was not the case. I was married for eight years, created two beautiful boys, but my fairytale ended. I was devastated. There was no one in my family that had ever been divorced. So how did I get here?

I honestly don't know the exact moment it started. When things changed, but I remember pleading for us to get help. I remember feeling like I was living a lie, because I would act happy when I was dying inside. The moment I saw myself in the mirror and no longer knew who I was, was the moment I knew I had to move on.

What would my family say? What would people think? So many thoughts going on at once. I was worried about my children, but finally worried about me.

So now what? I am now a single woman with two boys and a daughter from a previous relationship. Where do I go from here? How do I build from this broken place?

I had to go back to my parents. After them giving me away to him, he brought me back to them. I left their house to be a wife, and went from a wife, back to their house. I felt like a failure.

In all honesty, I was afraid. Will anyone want to be with a woman with three children? How can I do this thing alone? I haven't dated in years! I was still concerned about being in a relationship instead of worrying about healing. I was rushing to find someone to fill this void, because truth be told, he moved on so why can't I? I began crying out to the Lord, "Lord I want a companion; I want someone to tell me that I am beautiful; someone to open the door for me, someone to hold me when I feel low, someone to make me laugh, and someone to talk out my issues with. I miss that."

Shoot let's not forget for eight years I had a man lying beside me, "loving on me"...now nothing. "Lord come on now!" "You know I want to live holy, so you need to send me someone to quench these desires real quick?" Sorry, but I'm, just being real. You can't go from having "apple pie" everyday; some good "apple pie" at that, to getting none at all!"

So after I gave the Lord my grocery list, He sat me down and then asked me, "Are you free?" "What, Lord? Of course, I'm free. My husband is gone." He said, "No, you are not; you are still broken, and any man I send you, you will only see the one that hurt you. You will only see the pain and you will push him away." Ohhhhhhhh....

Now believe me, I know this is not an overnight thing. The healing takes time; it is a process. There is no book that can really show you how to overcome the pain. Every situation is different, but these words that I am sharing delivered me and I pray it will also deliver you. The Holy Spirit downloaded this to me one day while sitting by a pool watching my boys swim thinking about how our family is now broken and how we now have visitation instead of us all enjoying moments like these together. Then the Holy Spirit said Cherise it's time to see—Are You Free

A-Accept It

R-Release It

E-Expose It

Y-un**Y**oke It

O-Overcome It

U-Understand It

F-Flip It

R-Rebirth It

E-Employ It

E-Embark On It

Table of Contents

A-Accept It……………………………………………..Chapter 1

R-Release It……………………………………………Chapter 2

E-Expose It……………………………………………..Chapter 3

Y-unYoke It……………………………………………Chapter 4

O-Overcome It………………………………………..Chapter 5

U-Understand ………………………………………..Chapter 6

F-Flip It…………………………………………………..Chapter 7

R-Rebirth It…………………………………………….Chapter 8

E-Employ It…………………………………………….Chapter 9

E-Embark On It……………………………………….Chapter 10

1

Accept It

*A*ccept It-

You have to stop replaying what should have happened, what could have happened, and what didn't happen and to be able to start moving forward. Philippians 3:13 states, *"Brothers I do not consider that I have made it my own, but one thing I do FORGETTING what lies behind and straining forward to what lies ahead, I press on toward the goal for the prize of the upward call of God in Christ Jesus."*

The English Standard Version says, **"Straining"** forward which means that you have to work on it. It is not easy to stop replaying what shoulda, woulda, or coulda. I shoulda said I love you more. I coulda been a better listener. If he woulda said he was sorry then....

Instead of rehearsing what used to be, prepare for what is to be. You have to believe and know that God has greater. Romans 8:28 says that "...ALL things work together for our good...."yes even this thing is working for you. Also 2 Corinthians 5:17 states, "God makes ALL things new." Both Scripture references use the word ALL. Not some, not a little bit, but ALL. Not part of it, but ALL of it will work for your good.

I had to learn how to press the pause button on my thoughts when I found myself drifting back there. Back to that place of oh I remember when. No, the memories do not leave, but you can learn how to stop yourself from going back down that road and begin to make new memories.

So pause, accept this for what it is, and look forward to what is to come! Get ready for your new!

Have you really accepted it? Not what you are telling your friends to make them think that you got it all together, but have you really accepted it? Now take some time to list things that you know you need to accept. Then pray and allow the Holy Spirit to give you directions on how to do it. Journal what you hear Him speaking to you.

_____

_____

_____

_____

2

Release It

Forgive those involved. Matthew 6:14 states "For if you forgive other people when they sin against you, your heavenly father will also forgive you." I know it is not easy forgiving someone that hurt you so badly. Even now you are reading this rolling your eyes and saying *"Girl please, you don't know what they did to me."* Believe me I know! The scripture itself reads "forgive so that you can be forgiven. Where would we be if God had not forgiven us? I know that I have done and may still do some things that I need God's forgiveness for. I am so grateful that He is a loving and forgiving Father.

Unforgiveness actually can make you sick, literally; there are medical reports that will confirm this. A CNN report states that blaming others can ruin your health, and CBN News reported on the deadly consequences of unforgiveness. Dr. Steven Standiford, chief of surgery at the Cancer Treatment Centers of America, said that refusing to forgive makes people sick and keeps them that way.

Unforgiveness is not only affecting you emotionally, but physically as well.

They are living their life, and we are sitting here miserable. No ma'am and no sir! Holding on to bitterness, unforgiveness is only hurting us. We must release these people that we are holding on to. Holding onto unforgiveness only allows the enemy an entryway that causes us to be angry and depressed.

Not only do you need to forgive them, but you also need to forgive yourself. There may be some things that you felt like you've done that caused the marriage to end, and because of that you are beating yourself up about it. Believe me, I was not a saint in my marriage. I hurt my husband badly at the end of it. I was ready to for it to end and I did and said everything I could for it all to be over. After it was over I realized what all I had done and how he really did not deserve it. I had to apologize to him and then forgive myself for allowing the pain to take me to that place.

It got to place where we were like roommates. I wasn't speaking to him, and he wasn't speaking to me. I would pray Lord fix him, Lord get him together. In one of my prayer moments asking God to fix him, He says to me "You are still his wife and you must act as such." "If this thing ends you want it to end knowing you have done all that you could to make it work." Of course I gave God the side eye. "Wait what Lord? Can you not see what he's doing? Can you not see what's going on? Can you not just fix him first?" I had to repent for not being the wife that I was supposed to be even in the moments that things were rocky.

So you must repent also for what you have done as well. I had to stop and ask God to come into my heart and help me to forgive my husband and forgive myself. I could not do that on my own.

Pray with me this prayer...
"God I release (Person's Name) to You. I no longer want to hold unforgiveness and bitterness in my heart. Yes they hurt me, but I give this pain to You. I even ask that you bless them even now Lord. I repent for anything that I may have done to hurt them. I repent for any role I played for the demise of this marriage. I thank You Lord there is no condemnation in You and therefore I will not condemn myself. I want to live my best life now and not walk around holding grudges. Help me oh Lord to forgive, help me to let it go and leave it right here. Free me from bitterness and shame. Restore my heart

back to the place before the hurt and pain, In Jesus' name." Amen...and then we move on.

_____
_____
_____
_____
_____
_____
_____
_____
_____
_____
_____
_____
_____
_____
_____
_____
_____
_____
_____
_____
_____
_____
_____

3

Expose It

*E*xpose It-

Talk to someone about what you are feeling, do not keep it to yourself. We like to put on a mask around others and act like everything is okay when we are hurting and broken on the inside.

As a mother, I wanted to guard my children from seeing me in pain, because I knew they were trying to adjust to it too. Around my friends, I had to act like I was good. "Girl I'm good. I'm glad I can finally move on." Not!! Even though things were bad we still had 8 years together and two beautiful children. This was 8 years of my life. There is still hurt involved when letting go of something that you have known for so long.

It is harder to put on the facade of being OKAY than just admitting you're hurting and dealing with it. Please understand it is okay to cry; crying is cleansing. It doesn't mean you are weak, it means you are healing. I had a moment where I couldn't be strong anymore. This thing hurt! I just turned on the shower and locked myself in the bathroom and just cried. I mean cried like a baby. *Why me? Why now? How could he do this to me? I don't want to be here!* Have you ever had a moment where you literally throw a tantrum and then you wait for God to say something and there is silence? Well that is what happened.

It was like when a child throws a tantrum, you just watch them cut up. As soon as they realize it is not working they stop and move on to the next thing. I threw a major tantrum that day, after I was finished I washed my face and kept going. It was like the Lord was like, *"Are you done now? Okay great because we have work to do!"*

The one thing the enemy likes to do is to get you by yourself and have you throw your own pity party. A part of a **PIT**y party is the pit, and we are NOT going to allow the enemy to have us in a pit. When you feel yourself sinking, reach out to your accountability partner. Find someone that you can pray and talk it out with. Based on Wikipedia an accountability partner is a person who coaches another person by helping the other person keep a commitment. That is the educated version of your BFF, girlfriend, or prayer partner. Do not walk this thing out alone. If you don't have anyone in your life to talk to, seek professional help from a counselor or minister. We shy away from seeking help because we don't want people to think we are crazy, or we don't want people in our business. This is what the professionals are here for. It is hard to get out of that dark place alone…please talk to someone. I am so grateful for my sisters/friends that were there with me from the very beginning. I don't know where I would be without them there, sometimes just to be a listening ear and other times to be a shoulder.

In Georgia, when you have minor aged children you have to go to a parenting class to assist the children with the transition. In the class, the facilitator was explaining the signs of depression. I really wasn't paying attention because I wasn't depressed—so I thought. I was handling what I was dealt. I wasn't thinking about ending my life. After all, isn't that what depression leads to?

Well, I realized, as the facilitator begins to mention common signs of depression, everything on his list was what I was experiencing or had experienced and wasn't aware of it! I was depressed and had no clue. The facilitator stated that people with depression sleep a lot, I have no appetite, no interest in things they love, are irritable, and have a roller coaster of emotions. WOW, that is me!

Being a business owner, I thought some of the signs were due to the fact that I was working hard. I knew that I was unhappy, but not to the point of depression. I remember one day visiting my mother in-law and she asked me if I was okay. I told her that I was doing fine, although I really wasn't. She told me that my children need me and I have to do what is best for me to make sure that I am okay and will be here for my kids. She knew nothing about what was going on, because like I stated earlier I was good at putting on the mask like everything was okay, but she saw it. After that conversation is when I looked myself in the mirror as was devastated at what I saw. I was fading away. I was smaller then I had ever been. I knew it was time to take care of me, before I completely lost me, but still never tied any of this to being depressed.

Once I understood that all I was dealing with was tied together, I realized I was depressed and had been for quite some time.

I talked to a friend about it once I realized what I was dealing with. She explained that it would make sense knowing what I had been dealing with and suggested I seek help and get medicated. Medicated!!! Oh no ma'am I was not in agreement with that! Now doctors are here to help as I said before and if you feel that you are depressed, please seek help.

There are so many people that are walking around depressed and have no clue until it is too late, but for me I was not accepting that I was depressed or needed to be medicated for depression. I went right into prayer..."*Lord I thank You for all that You are doing in my life. I praise You for being a loving Father, for being my Lover and Best Friend, for keeping me when I did not know how to keep myself, for keeping my mind in moments when I wanted to give up. I come against the spirit of depression right now, in the name of Jesus! Depression has no authority in this body. Lord in Your word You said that You have given me authority to tread upon serpents and scorpions, and ALL the powers of the enemy, and*
NOTHING shall hurt me! Therefore I rebuke every attack of my mind to cause me to feel low. I rebuke the spirit of rejection and bitterness in Jesus name! My body is the temple of the Holy Ghost therefore nothing can be in this body that is not of Christ. If there is It Is there illegally and MUST flee in Jesus name!" Amen.

Once you expose the enemy the enemy must flee! James 4:7

From that day forward I walked in freedom over the spirit of depression! I was free!

4
UnYoke It

UnYoke It-

Ephesians 5:31 *"For this reason a man will leave his father and mother and will cleave to his wife and the two will become one flesh."* When you give yourself to someone sexually, the two of you become one. This is what they call "Soul Ties". Business Coach Linda Dominique Grosvenor-Holland has a book titled, *Breaking Soul Ties, How to take your whole heart with you when love is ove*r; this book breaks down in detail what a Soul Tie is.

Even though you may no longer be with the person you are still tied to them because your souls became one. In order to move forward, you have to break this tie. My pastor gave this example: If you were to glue two pieces of paper together and then pull them apart, some of the paper will still be stuck to the other. Although you have separated, there are still parts of you with that person. You must pray for all ties to be broken.

Pray this prayer with me…

"Lord I belong to You, I pray that You'll cleanse me now in Jesus name from every soul tie. Release me from this soul connection with (Persons Name). Free me from any entanglement in the spirit in Jesus name. Reveal to me anything that I may be holding on to that is still keeping me tied to this person. I pray that I am free so that the mate that You have for me can receive me. In Jesus name, I pray." Amen!

So once you have cleansed yourself spiritually, it is now time to clean up physically. Why are you still holding on to that night shirt he slept in, or those letters she wrote you? Get rid of ALL things that tie you to that person. If it is hard for you to let go, call a friend over to help you. Make it a party! Turn on some music, get some trash bags and get to cleaning!!

_____
_____
_____
_____
_____
_____
_____

5
Overcome It

*O*vercome It-

The definition of overcome is: *to get the better of a struggle.* Get the better of this thing! Don't let it get the best of you! Philippians 4:13 "I can do ALL things through Christ who gives me strength." Pull from that strength. You are an overcomer! You can get through this! I had to pull from the strength of the Lord at this time in my life...for real. Remember I had to move back in with my parents with my three children.

I am a thirty-five year old woman with three children now living with my parents...really?! My husband was the main bread winner of the family. I had a t-shirt business, but that income was not constant, so I struggled financially.

I saw my children hurting, which of course hurt me. Realizing that everything that I knew to be my life for eight years was over weighed heavily on me, but I had to overcome. I had to make the best of where I was in life. I was determined to work hard as well as better myself so that I could have better for me and my children. Each day became easier and easier until I looked up and realized it was not a struggle anymore. You can overcome it!

6

Understand It

Understand It-

Do a self-check...look within to see what areas you need to fix in you in order to move forward. Let's not continue to focus on what he or she did or didn't do. It is time to look at self. If you know you get attitudes quickly, which caused a conflict in your relationship, let's check that. For me, I didn't communicate. I would shut down and not express what I felt. I knew I needed to deal with that. Also I didn't cook because my husband did.

I needed to make sure I could cook my new mate a good meal, so I started creating a menu for the week of new dishes that I could learn to cook. We have to work on us. Stop pointing the finger and look within. Galatians 6:4 reads "But each one must examine his work, and then he will have reason for boasting in regards to himself alone, and not in regard to another."

The scripture says it all, look at yourself, and get yourself right so at the end you can boast! We all know that there is that part of us that when our ex sees us, we want them to wish they never left.

Well if we are walking around looking broke, busted, and disgusted, we don't have too much to boast about. Really though "Understand It", do a self evaluation. What are some things that you need to work on to make you better? Maybe it is working out or just taking time out for you. I personally took this time to really reconnect with the Father, spending more time in His presence and learning from Him. He then began to reveal to me those things that needed healing and what I needed deliverance from. Sometimes taking the blinders off and seeing who you really are can be painful, but allowing Him to come in and restore and refill you is worth the process.

What are some things that you know you need to work on to make an even better you and what are you going to do about it?

_____

_____

_____

_____

7
Flip It

lip It-

It is time to stop with the "woe is me" lingo. Understand, as stated earlier, that "ALL things work together for your good..." (Romans 8:28). Yes, even this is working for your good. You might be saying, *really Cherise?* How can my marriage ending work for my good? My life has changed from what I knew it to be. Believe me, I was there. "Lord what is this about?" "How do I recover from this?"

How is this working for my good? Because of what I went through I am now helping others to get through. This pain that I went through, this process was for His divine purpose. It also worked for my good because it brought me back to Him. Not only that, but it allowed me to find a love that was created just for me. Yes, I was able to love again! You can too! Find **your** good!

_____

_____

_____

8
Rebirth It

*R*ebirth It-

What does that mean to you? Find yourself again. At times when we get in relationships, we will lose ourselves in it trying to be what that person wants us to be. We put our dreams and visions on hold to make sure that our family is happy. Years down the line we look up and don't know what happened. What happened to my dreams? Where did my passion and drive go for that thing that I use to love to do?

I loved writing plays. I had so many dreams and visions that just faded away. I had a t-shirt business that brought me so much joy and did so well, but I lost the love for that. I had to get that person back. Where is that person that loved to laugh? What happened to the person that enjoyed writing? Where did she go? I had to get her back.

Everything that has been laying dormant in you, every gift and talent, I pray will be resurrected now in Jesus name.

I thank You Lord that the person reading this will rebirth those things that they let sit. Those desires that You placed inside of them, the very thing that they put on the back burner, let them go back and get it. In Jesus name! Let the books come forth, let the business come forth. Let them have the push to register for school. Stir it up of God!!

What are some things that you put on the back burner? Make it a goal to at least start one of those things this week.

_____
_____
_____
_____
_____
_____
_____
_____
_____
_____
_____
_____
_____

9
Employ It

*E*mploy It-

Get to work! Get busy! Enjoy this time doing something that you've always wanted to do. Let your pain employ you to help someone else who may be going through what you went through. Let your story be their encouragement.

Listen! I never saw myself writing a book…especially about divorce, but God had a different plan and this very book will help millions of people. Oh wow, that's what the Holy Spirit had me write…millions! Let your story help millions! Let this time work for you. Nothing we go through is just for us, for your very testimony can help someone who was on the verge of giving up on it all. There are more books to be written, more podcasts to host, more conferences to do.

Get ready to let your pain employ you!

List some things the Holy Spirit has given you that you know would help someone else:

10
Embark It

*E*mbark On It-

At this moment you have accepted it, released it, exposed it, unyoked it, overcome it, understood it, flipped it, rebirthed it, employed it, and now you are embarking on it. This is now who you are, so what do you do? It is time to love you. Love yourself again; spend time getting to know you again.

You have allowed God to come in and heal your heart. You let Him show you real love, that unconditional, non judgmental love that sustains our soul. He gives the type of love that never leaves, that love that never changes, that love that only He can give.

One thing, that I had to do, was to let Him back into my heart. Honestly I did not know that He wasn't in my heart until one day I was worshipping and He said, *"You have not fully let Me in. You are guarding your heart from being hurt therefore you have also guarded it from letting Me come in."* Wow!! That wall that I put up so that no one could get in and hurt me again also blocked the Father out too.

Let's pray:

Lord I welcome You back into my heart and make my heart pliable. Where I may have hardened it from pain and disappoint, bring that stony heart back to a heart of flesh. Let me embark on this new time in my life. Let me not look back on yesterday's heartache, but focus on the opportunities of tomorrow. Prepare me for what is to come, and order my footsteps Lord. Continue to prepare me to be who You have called me to be. I am ready to take this walk of singleness with you walking with me Lord.

Now I will be honest, I had to go through the steps a few times before I was able to completely move on. You will know when you are really ready to embark on your new. My new came out of nowhere. The moment I wasn't looking for anything, but focusing on what God had called me to is when my King came. Yes y'all I truly became free and was able to love again!

There were still wounds there that I did not know were there until he came along, but he was patient with me and walked me through the healing. I truly believe that there are wounds that only your lover love can heal. This man that God sent for me spoke life to ever dead place. He made love exciting for me again.

I am now embarking on a new adventure with my King and my Father! This can be your testimony to!

Take some time to journal your feelings and thoughts after reading this book.

_____

_____

_____

_____

_____

_____

_____

_____

_____

_____

_____

_____

_____

Depression is a very serious disease. Many like myself, have walked with it and had no clue that they are dealing with it, while others are battling with it alone. Please see the signs, and if you or someone you know has these symptoms please seek help.

Symptoms

Prolonged sadness or unexplained crying spells

Significant changes in appetite and sleep patterns

Irritability, anger, worry, agitation, anxiety

Pessimism, indifference

Loss of energy, persistent lethargy

Feelings of guilt, worthlessness

Inability to concentrate, indecisiveness

Inability to take pleasure in former interests, social withdrawal

Unexplained aches and pains

Recurring thoughts of death or suicide

Free Resources

Suicide

Suicide Hotline

1-800-SUICIDE

National Suicide Prevention Helpline

1-800-273-TALK

National Adolescent Suicide Hotline

1-800-621-4000

Depression

Postpartum Depression

1-800-PPD-MOMS

Veterans

1-877-VET2VET

About The Author

Cherise Parker..Author, Entrepreneur, Prophetic Worshiper, Lover of God...

Walking for years not knowing my purpose or who I was. I dealt with feelings of low self worth, rejection, and low self esteem I had to overcome the negative labels that society created for me. I AM divorced. I AM broke. I AM depressed. I AM alone and I had to realize the most powerful words come behind your I AM.

Divorced and seeking to find my identity in Christ, the Lord birth out of me I AM...The Movement and I AM M.E. (made excellent)™ I AM now on a mission to reach the hearts of women and young ladies around the world to help remove the labels that society has given them. I AM focused on getting them to see who they are in Christ. When you receive The Great I AM and understand that The Great I AM is in you, you will be able to see how great you really are!

www.ingramcontent.com/pod-product-compliance
Lightning Source LLC
Chambersburg PA
CBHW071802040426
42446CB00012B/2678